Macmillan/McGraw-Hill TIMELINKS

All Together

PROGRAM AUTHORS
James A. Banks
Kevin P. Colleary
Linda Greenow
Walter C. Parker
Emily M. Schell
Dinah Zike

CONTRIBUTORS
Raymond C. Jones
Irma M. Olmedo

 Macmillan/McGraw-Hill

Culture

Students with print disabilities may be eligible to obtain an accessible, audio version of the pupil edition of this textbook. Please call Recording for the Blind & Dyslexic at 1-800-221-4792 for complete information.

The McGraw·Hill Companies

Macmillan
McGraw-Hill

Copyright © 2009 by The McGraw-Hill Companies, Inc. All rights reserved. Except as permitted under the United States Copyright Act, no part of this publication may be reproduced or distributed in any form or by any means, or stored in a database or retrieval system, without prior permission of the publisher.
Send all inquires to: Macmillan/McGraw-Hill, 8787 Orion Place, Columbus, OH 43240-4027

MHID 0-02-151344-9   ISBN 978-0-02-151344-4   Printed in the United States of America

4 5 6 7 8 9 10 WVR/LEH 13 12 11 10

All Together

Table of Contents

Skills and Features

Maps

Families and Neighbors

People, Places, and Events

Ashley's Family

Ashley's family likes to be together.

Eagle Park

Eagle Park has a lake, swings, slides, and picnic tables.

Ashley's Family Picnic

Come to our Family Picnic on Saturday.

Ashley's family has a special **picnic** in Eagle Park every year.

Our Families

Lesson 1

Vocabulary

family

rule

Reading Skill

Retell

Detail
Detail
Detail

4

Families at Home

Our **family** is made up of the people we love. Families take care of each other and have fun together.

Some families are big. Some families are small. Families come in many shapes and sizes.

 What is a family?

Places
Amusement Park

David goes on a ride with his brother and grandma. They have fun riding the roller coaster together!

Families Help Each Other

Jake lives with his dad and aunt. They each have work to do. Jake vacuums the living room rug. His dad cooks dinner. His aunt washes the dishes.

Families follow **rules**. Rules tell us what we can and cannot do. One rule in Jake's family is to wash your hands before eating.

 What is one rule in Jake's family?

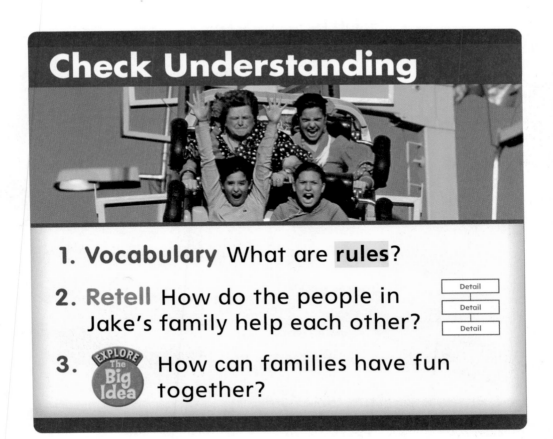

Check Understanding

1. **Vocabulary** What are **rules**?

2. **Retell** How do the people in Jake's family help each other?

Detail
Detail
Detail

3. **EXPLORE The Big Idea** How can families have fun together?

Use Addresses

Vocabulary

address

Every home has an **address**. The first part is a number. The second part is a street name. Hector lives at 4 Pine Street.

Pine Street

4

Mia lives in the red house. The red house is next to Hector's house.

Pine Street

2 4 6

Try the Skill

1. What parts make up an address?

2. What is Mia's address?

✏️ **Writing Activity**
Draw where you live. Write the number by the door. Write your address below the picture.

Families Together

Lesson 2

Vocabulary

custom

celebrate

Reading Skill

Retell

Detail

Detail

Detail

Families Have Customs

Every year after the family picnic, Ashley's grandma opens a sewing box. Together, the family adds a new patch to their family quilt. This is a **custom** in Ashley's family. A custom is a special way of doing something.

 What is a custom?

Event
Moving the Sheep

Marie's family has a special custom. Every September they help Mr. Banks move his sheep to greener pastures. Then they celebrate. They eat, sing songs, and dance.

Families Celebrate

It is a custom in many families to **celebrate** birthdays. Celebrate means to show happiness about a thing or event.

Ryan's family has a special custom. Each spring, they go together to the Seneca Zoo in Rochester, New York.

They celebrate the birth of the new baby animals. This year, Ryan's family celebrated the birth of two baby tigers!

 What is Ryan's family custom?

Check Understanding

1. **Vocabulary** What does the word **celebrate** mean?

2. **Retell** What is Ryan's family custom?

Detail
Detail
Detail

3. What customs do you have in your family?

Citizenship

Points of View

How does your family celebrate?

These first graders are from Jericho, New York. Read about how they celebrate birthdays.

Jericho, New York

"My family sings 'Happy Birthday' in Hebrew and in English. My grandma makes a special cake that has no flour in it because my birthday is at Passover. We can't eat bread then."

Benjamin Alon

Benjamin Alon

"On my birthday my friends come over and I wear my special Chinese red gown. I play with my friends. We also eat Chinese candy."

Nadine Wang

Nadine Wang

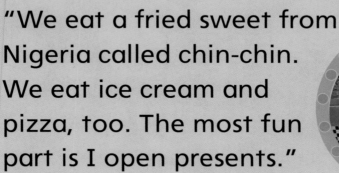

"We eat a fried sweet from Nigeria called chin-chin. We eat ice cream and pizza, too. The most fun part is I open presents."

Ikenna Ajah

Ikenna Ajah

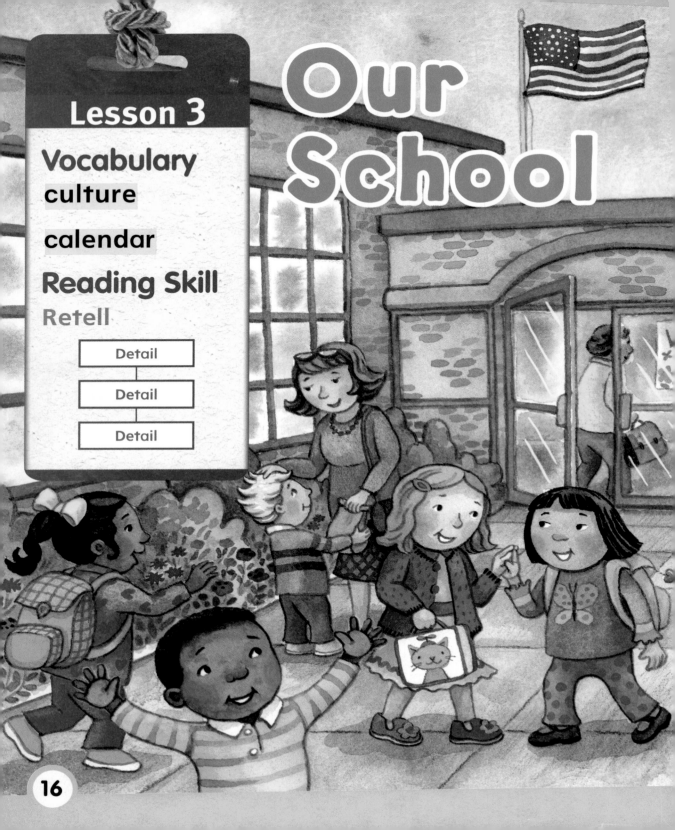

Lesson 3

Vocabulary
culture

calendar

Reading Skill
Retell

| Detail |
| Detail |
| Detail |

Our School

What Is School?

School can be a wonderful place.
In school we learn to read and write.
We find out about numbers and far
away places.

Together, we learn to play new
games. We learn to get along with
each other. We make new friends!

 What can you do in school?

Rules at School

In school we follow rules, just like at home. One school rule is to stay to the right when you walk down the hallway. This rule keeps us from bumping into one another.

We need rules in the classroom, too. One classroom rule is to raise your hand when you want to speak. This rule gives everyone in class a turn to speak and be heard.

 What is a rule in your classroom?

A Class Celebration

Ben's class celebrates many **cultures**. Culture means the special food, music, and art of a group of people.

This **calendar** shows when Ben's class will have Culture Day. A calendar is a chart that shows the months, weeks, and days of a year.

SEPTEMBER

Sunday	Monday	Tuesday	Wednesday	Thursday	Friday	Saturday
		1	2	3	4	5
6	7 School Begins	8	9	10	11	12
13	14	15	16	17 Open School Night	18	19
20	21 Fall Begins	22	23	24	25	26
27	28	29	30 Culture Day			

On Culture Day, children tell about their family's culture. They play games from around the world. They sing songs in different languages.

 What does a calendar show?

Check Understanding

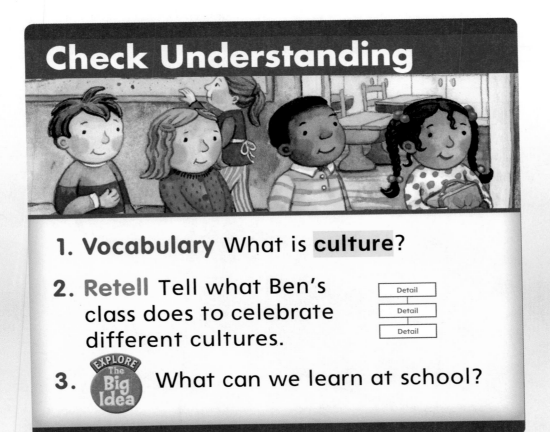

1. **Vocabulary** What is **culture**?

2. **Retell** Tell what Ben's class does to celebrate different cultures.

Detail
Detail
Detail

3. **EXPLORE The Big Idea** What can we learn at school?

Our Neighbors

Lesson 4

Vocabulary

neighbor

neighborhood

Reading Skill

Retell

Detail
Detail
Detail

In a Neighborhood

People who live near each other are called **neighbors**. They live together in a **neighborhood**.

Neighbors can share food from their gardens. They can help each other keep their neighborhood clean.

 How can neighbors help?

People
Jane Addams

Jane Addams opened her house to neighbors who needed help. She called it Hull-House. She said, "All the people in the world are neighbors."

mancala

New Neighbors

Lisa has a new neighbor named Chanya. Chanya's family came from East Africa. They moved into the house next door to Lisa.

Chanya taught Lisa a game called *mancala*. It is an African game played with small beads.

Lisa invited Chanya to join her Brownie troop. They also sing together in the school choir. Lisa is happy to have her new neighbor!

mancala beads

 What is *mancala*?

Check Understanding

1. **Vocabulary** What is a **neighborhood**?

2. **Retell** What happened when Chanya moved into Lisa's neighborhood?

Detail
Detail
Detail

3. **EXPLORE The Big Idea** Who are your neighbors?

Lesson 5

Reading Skill

Retell

| Detail |
| Detail |
| Detail |

America
Is Special

Many Lands

People came to America from all over the world. They brought special foods. They brought fun games, dances, and songs and customs!

 What are some things people brought to America?

soccer

Irish step dance

Many Cultures

We may wear different clothes. We may speak different languages. But, the words "Hello, my friend," are spoken in every language!

Around the World

This child lives in Australia. In Australia they have a special custom. First, they paint their bodies. Then, they dance and tell a family story.

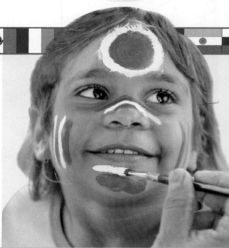

Our families, neighborhoods, and schools are made up of people from all over the world. We came from many different cultures.

 How are we alike and different?

Check Understanding

1. **Vocabulary** What are different ways we can say "Hello"?

2. **Retell** What did you learn about other cultures?

Detail
Detail
Detail

3. How is America special?

Vocabulary

Complete each sentence.

rule   neighbor   calendar

1. A person who lives near you is called a _____.

2. A chart that shows the months, weeks, and days is called a _____.

3. A _____ is something that tells us what we can and cannot do.

Critical Thinking

4. Why are rules important?

5. What is a special custom in your family?

Map and Globe Skills

Use Addresses

Look at the picture of downtown Redville. Answer the question below.

6. What is the address of the Post Office?

A. 5 Elm Street

B. 7 Elm Street

C. 9 Elm Street

Culture Activity

Make a Customs Book

1 Fold two sheets of paper. Tape them together.

2 Draw one picture to show a different custom on each fold.

3 Write a label under each picture.

4 Share your book with the class.

A New Kid on the Block

Characters

Tina

Matt

Hala

Angelo

Narrator Tina, Matt, and Hala are friends. There is a block party in their neighborhood today. They meet to have fun together. Angelo is new in the neighborhood. His family just moved here from Italy.

Tina Hi, Matt. Have a hot dog!

Matt Hi, Tina. Isn't this a great block party? Look, there's Hala.

Hala Hi, pals! Let's play Four Square!

Tina Four Square? But we need four players. Maybe we can find somebody to play.

Matt Hey, isn't that the new boy? Maybe he would play with us.

Hala I don't know. We don't even know him.

Matt So what? Let's ask him to play. Hi, my name is Matt. What is yours?

Angelo My name is Angelo.

Matt Angelo, these are my friends Hala and Tina.

Tina Hi, Angelo. Do you want to play Four Square with us?

Angelo Sure! But I do not know how to play.

Tina Do not worry. We can show you!

Narrator Angelo and his new friends play Four Square all afternoon.

Hala Now I am hungry again!

Tina All of the good food is gone!

Angelo I have an idea! I'll be right back.

Narrator Angelo goes into his apartment. Soon he comes out holding a plate.

Hala Yum! Those look good! What are they?

Angelo They are called strufoli. My mom made them for the block party.

Hala They are great! Can I have more?

Angelo Sure. My mom made enough for everyone.

Narrator Hala, Tina, and Matt are so happy to have their new friend, Angelo. The block party ends too soon for all of them.

Tina I have to go home now. School is tomorrow.

Matt Thanks for playing with us, Angelo.

Angelo Thanks for showing me how to play Four Square! I'll see you in school tomorrow.

Hala Okay. Could you try to bring us more of that yummy strufoli? (laughing)

Readers Theater Activity

How did Tina, Matt, and Hala help Angelo feel welcome? What could you do to make a new child feel welcome? First, draw a picture of your idea. Then, act it out.

Share my apple.

Picture Glossary

A

address An **address** is the number and street where someone lives. (page 8)

C

calendar A **calendar** is a chart that shows the months, weeks, and days of a year. (page 20)

celebrate **Celebrate** means to show happiness about a thing or an event. (page 12)

culture **Culture** is the special food, music, and art of a group of people. (page 20)

custom A **custom** is a special way of doing something. (page 11)

F

family A **family** is made up of the people we love. (page 5)

N

neighbor A **neighbor** is a person who lives near you. (page 23)

neighborhood A **neighborhood** is a place where people live together. (page 23)

R

rule A **rule** tells us what we can and cannot do. (page 7)

Index

This index lists many things you can find in your book. It tells the page numbers on which they are found. If you see the letter *m* before a page number, you will find a map on that page.

Credits

Maps: XNR

Illustrations: 8: Sally Vitsky. 9: Sally Vitsky. 14-15: Sarah Dillard. 16: Maggie Smith. 18: Maggie Smith. 20: Shirley Beckes. 22: Hector Borlasca. 28: Hideko Takahashi. 31: Viviana Garofoli.

Photography Credits: All Photographs are by Macmillan/McGraw-hill (MMH) except as noted below.

John Henley/CORBIS. 2: (bkgd) Masterfile; (c) Ken Karp for MMH. 3: (b) Yellow Dog Productions/Getty Images; (t) image100/PunchStock. 4: Rob Lewine/CORBIS. 5: Gernot Huber/Laif/Aurora Photos. 6: CORBIS/PunchStock. 7: (b) Gernot Huber/Laif/Aurora Photos; (t) Grace/zefa/CORBIS. 10: (bkgd) Masterfile; (fg) Ken Karp for MMH. 11: (b) Purestock/SuperStock; (t) Ken Karp for MMH. 12: Peter Steiner/Alamy Images. 13: (c) Ken Karp for MMH; (t) Peter Arnold, Inc./ Schafer & Hill/Alamy Images. 14: (l) Susan Menkes/Cantiague Elementary School. 15: (br) Susan Menkes/Cantiague Elementary School; (tl) Ilgar Guo. 17: (tl) SW Productions/Getty Images; (tr) Getty Images. 19: Steve Chenn/CORBIS. 20: (bl) Patrick Olear/PhotoEdit. 21: (t) Steve Cole/Getty Images. 23: (b) 1996 Image Farm, Inc.; (inset) SuperStock. 24: Ken Karp for MMH. 25: (t) Ken Karp for MMH. 26: Ariel Skelley/CORBIS. 27: (l) Tim Pannell/CORBIS; (r) Kayte M. Deioma/PhotoEdit. 28: (b) Bill Bachman. 29: Tim Pannell/CORBIS. 30: Ken Karp for MMH. 32: (t) Stockdisc Classic/Alamy Images. 33: (cl) Blend Images/PunchStock; (cr) Blend Images/PunchStock; (l) Blend Images/PunchStock; (r) Blend Images/PunchStock. 34: (bc) Blend Images/PunchStock; (bl) Blend Images/PunchStock; (br) Blend Images/PunchStock; (t) John A Rizzo/Getty Images. 35: (b) SuperStock/Jupiterimages. 36: PhotoLink/Getty Images. 37: (bl) Blend Images/PunchStock; (br) DEA/PRIMA PRESS/De Agostini Editore Picture Library. 39: Blend Images/PunchStock. R1: (b) Patrick Olear/PhotoEdit; (bc) Rob Lewine/CORBIS. R2: (c) John Henley/CORBIS; (t) Ken Karp for MMH; (tc) Rob Lewine/CORBIS.